MODERN TRACTION IN THE NORTH OF ENGLAND

JOHN WHITELEY

AMBERLEY

First published 2024

Amberley Publishing
The Hill, Stroud
Gloucestershire, GL5 4EP

www.amberley-books.com

Copyright © John Whiteley, 2024

The right of John Whiteley to be identified as
the Author of this work has been asserted in
accordance with the Copyrights, Designs and
Patents Act 1988.

ISBN 978 1 3981 1662 7 (print)
ISBN 978 1 3981 1663 4 (ebook)

British Library Cataloguing in Publication Data.
A catalogue record for this book is available from
the British Library.

Typesetting by SJmagic DESIGN SERVICES, India.
Printed in the UK.

Introduction

Ever since I can remember I have had a passion for railways, much to the bewilderment of first my parents, and latterly my own family. How it came about, I really don't know as I am not from a family who worked on the railways, having merely had a distant older cousin who was a fireman at Low Moor steam shed. I do remember he promised me a ride on the footplate when I was a bit older, but he moved from the railways when the first diesel multiple units started to appear, so I never got that ride.

Having attended junior school at Lightcliffe, near Halifax, I subsequently got a place at Whitcliffe Mount Grammar School at Cleckheaton, not far from where I was then living at Lightcliffe. Whilst at grammar school I became interested in photography, and left at the age of sixteen with an undistinguished academic record, probably due to my increased interest in railways at the expense of studies. However, I did eventually manage to get five GCE O levels, which enabled me to sit professional exams as a chartered surveyor. After leaving school I worked at an architects and surveyors office in Dewsbury for about three years. I then had another two years or so working as a trainee valuer at the District Valuers Office in Bradford, after which I got a job in private practice in Bradford with a firm of chartered surveyors, having finally qualified as a chartered surveyor in 1967. After a few years I became a partner in the firm where I remained until retirement, and for the last thirty years or so of my working life, being self-employed, it gave me the freedom to pursue my hobby at times during the working week.

From early 1961 until December 1963 I used a fixed-lens 35 mm Yashica camera for black and white photography and did my own processing, but how I wish I could have afforded to use the more expensive colour film in those days. Sadly my meagre income then would only allow me to purchase the occasional roll of black and white film, as other expenses included the cost of entry to Thrum Hall to support Halifax Rugby League team, expenditure on girlfriends at the time and attempting to boost the profits of local breweries. Happy days indeed – oh to do it all again!

Although my early photography was mainly steam, fortunately I did also record modern traction, both locally and also elsewhere in the UK. One Saturday in June 1961 I travelled by train to Hensall on the line to Goole, and then walked the short distance to near Heck on the East Coast Main Line. One of the first trains I photographed was a Deltic speeding south on the 'Flying Scotsman', the sight of which and the sound of the twin Napier engines impressed me immensely and was probably the catalyst for all the modern traction photography I have done ever since.

I did eventually start using colour film in 1966, initially with Pentax 35 mm cameras and Kodachrome 25 film and later Nikon 35 mm cameras with Provia 100F film before going digital in around 2011. However, in common with many other photographers, when steam finished in the UK in 1968, I regularly went overseas to photograph foreign steam. Although my many overseas trips have been most enjoyable, those made in the late 1960s and early 1970s were partly at the expense of photographing modern traction in the UK, something which I now regret in an ever-changing railway scene.

Putting this book together has been a most enjoyable exercise as it has given me the opportunity to trawl through tens of thousands of modern traction slides in my collection, many of which I would otherwise probably have never seen again.

At Clay Cross, about 4 miles south of Chesterfield, the line to Birmingham via Derby separates from the line to Trent and Leicester, which passes Toton Yard. On Tuesday 16 May 1989 Class 47/3 No. 47302, in its attractive Railfreight red stripe colours, comes off the Toton line heading north with a train of 100-ton bogie tanks.

A pair of Class 37/5s in Railfreight red stripe colours, Nos 37517 and 37514, are rounding the corner off the Birmingham line heading a Margam–Tees Yard steel train on Tuesday 16 May 1989 as Class 47/4 No. 47536 in large logo blue livery approaches on the afternoon Newcastle–Plymouth vans.

Looking smart in its large logo blue livery, Class 47/4 No. 47665 is passing Clay Cross South Junction heading the 12.03 Poole–Newcastle towards its next stop at Chesterfield on Wednesday 10 May 1989.

On 11 July 1989 Railfreight-liveried Class 58 No. 58047 is heading a heavy train of HAA Merry-go-Round (MGR) coal hoppers towards Toton as a Sheffield–St Pancras InterCity HST is overtaking on the approach to Clay Cross on 11 July 1989. Built in October 1986, No. 58047 was destined to be one of several Class 58s to be exported via the Channel Tunnel for use in mainland Europe.

Class 47/0 No. 47085 *Conidae* is nearing Chesterfield at Hasland on 3 July 1989 heading the 13.15 Grange Junction–Tees oil tanks. After the new Railfreight sectors had been introduced in 1987, No. 47085 is sporting the Railfreight Petroleum livery.

Looking rather weather stained on Sunday 9 June 1968, BR Peak No. D38 is heading south near Hasland after its stop at Chesterfield heading 1M92, an afternoon Sheffield–St Pancras express. The first ten of these BR/Sulzer Type 4s, built in 1959/60, were named after English and Welsh mountains, hence they were quickly dubbed the 'Peaks'. No. D38 would be renumbered 45032 in March 1975 and was withdrawn from Tinsley in May 1981 having had twenty years in service.

Class 37/5s Nos 37679 and 37687 are heading south from Chesterfield, its distinctive crooked parish church spire visible in the distance. No. 37679 is in Railfreight red stripe livery and No. 37687 is in Railfreight Construction livery and they are heading the Earles–Handsworth cement on Wednesday 10 May 1989.

On Monday 1 September 1975 an unidentified Peak is leaving Chesterfield with 1M86, a Glasgow–St Pancras express which had been named the 'Thames-Clyde Express' until May 1974 when the train lost its title.

Specially painted by Toton depot with its white cab roof and red buffer beam, Peak Class 45/1 No. 45114 looks very smart as it leaves Sheffield with the 15.00 to St Pancras on Saturday 15 September 1979.

The Class 76 electric locomotives were built in 1950 specifically for the 1,500Vdc Manchester–Sheffield overhead electrification. Huge amounts of coal were carried on this line from the Yorkshire coal fields to Lancashire via the Woodhead Tunnel. On Thursday 21 September 1978 No. 76049 has just passed the remains of Sheffield Victoria, which had closed in January 1970, with returning coal empties.

On Saturday 21 April 1979 a pair of Class 76 electrics converted to multiple working and air braking were used between Guide Bridge and Tinsley Yard on the 'Woldsman Rail Tour' organised by the LCGB, which ran from Liverpool to Cleethorpes. Nos 76014 and 76030 are arriving at Tinsley Yard at about 11.35 where a pair of Class 31s took over for the run to Cleethorpes.

Class 76 No. 76041 with its pantographs raised to their maximum height is passing Penistone station on Wednesday 7 September 1977 with a general freight returning from Lancashire to Tinsley Yard. The line diverging to the right is to Barnsley and Huddersfield.

A sad sight on Wednesday 27 April 1983 as Class 37/0 No. 37265 nears Chinley hauling Class 76 electrics Nos 76054, 76010 and 76039, which are destined for breaking up at C. F. Booth in Rotherham.

Peak Class 45/0 No. 45019 with refurbished front end is near Woodburn Junction as it leaves Sheffield on Saturday 10 December 1983 with a footex from Sheffield to Lincoln.

Class 37/0 No. 37246 is passing New Mills South Junction signal box on Tuesday 3 April 1984 heading a long train of empty Presflo cement wagons from Northenden to Earles Sidings in the Hope Valley.

Also on Tuesday 3 April 1984 Peak Class 45/0 No. 45001 has just passed Chinley heading a limestone train from Peak Forest to the ICI Lostock Works at Northwich as a Class 124 Trans-Pennine unit slows for its station stop.

In the early 1980s pairs of Class 37s were progressively replacing the older Class 40s on heavy Peak Forest stone trains. On 11 August 1983 Class 37/0s Nos 37128 and 37086 are reversing Peakstone empties into the sidings as English Electric Class 40 No. 40150 stands at the signal.

In 1983–84 Class 31s started to be used on locomotive-hauled trains replacing some life-expired diesel multiple units. One such service using the later Class 31/4s was from Humberside and Sheffield to Manchester and Liverpool via the Hope Valley. On Saturday 10 November 1984 a Class 31/4 is nearing Chinley North Junction on a Manchester–Hull train.

Peak Class 45/1 No. 45105 has come round the sharp corner at Holmes Junction having just left Rotherham Masborough heading the 09.35 Carlisle–Nottingham on Saturday 21 April 1979. The line to the right leads into Booth's scrapyard. Rotherham Masborough station was to close in 1988 when services were moved to Rotherham Central.

On Tuesday 5 May 1987 Class 47/4 No. 47664 is passing Kilnhurst, a few miles north of Rotherham, heading the 09.33 Penzance–Newcastle. In the background is Kilnhurst Colliery, which closed in 1989.

On Wednesday 18 March 1987 Peak Class 45/0 No. 45041 is taking the Doncaster line past the yards at Knottingley with a train of wagons for repair. Knottingley station on the line to Goole is in the background with a diesel multiple unit awaiting departure.

Between 1985 and 1995 General Motors in North America built fifteen Class 59 locomotives for heavy freight use. National Power based at Ferrybridge acquired six between 1994 and 1995, initially for coal and gypsum traffic, and as Class 59/2 adopted a stunning livery of mid-blue with matching coloured hoppers. On Thursday 7 March 1996 No. 59201 *Vale of York* rounds the corner at Knottingley with a block coal train from Gascoigne Wood to Drax Power Station, with Ferrybridge Power Station in the background.

National Power sold their entire rail operation to English Welsh and Scottish Railway (EWS) in 1998 and the original blue livery was replaced by the standard EWS maroon and gold. On 27 August 1998 Class 59/2 No. 59201 *Vale of York* is nearing Knottingley as it returns from Drax to Gascoigne Wood. It is still carrying its presentation bell and the empty hoppers are still in National Power colours.

On Thursday 19 March 1987, at a time when there was an insatiable demand for coal at the three Aire Valley power stations, Class 56 No. 56007 in Railfreight large logo grey is passing Knottingley depot with empties returning to Gascoigne Wood from either Eggborough or Drax. No. 56007 was one of thirty Class 56s built in Romania and was one of thirty hired by Fertis in France between September 2005 and November 2006 for use on construction trains on the new high-speed line between Paris and Strasbourg.

Tuesday 27 February 1996 was a cold morning of very little wind resulting in huge plumes of steam from both Eggborough Power Station on the left and Drax Power Station in the distance on the right. National Power Class 59/2 No. 59203 *Vale of Pickering* is easing its train of empty hoppers from Eggborough on to the main line at Whitley Bridge Junction.

Following the success of the prototype English Electric Deltic, an order was placed in 1958 for twenty-two similar production locomotives to replace steam on East Coast Main Line express passenger services. My very first photograph of an English Electric Deltic was taken on Saturday 17 June 1961 when one raced south near Heck heading the Up 'Flying Scotsman'. I didn't record its number, but at the time there were only six in service, Nos D9000–D9005.

When Selby was still on the East Coast Main Line before the Selby diversion was built in 1983, on Thursday 13 December 1962, Deltic No. D9007, later No. 55007 and named *Pinza*, is passing through the station heading the Down 'Flying Scotsman'.

A picture taken from the signal box on the swing bridge above the River Ouse on Sunday 22 March 1964. An unidentified Deltic has just passed through Selby station and is crossing the bridge heading a Down express. It is still in its original BR two-tone green livery, but now has small yellow warning panels.

Due to possible subsidence caused by the newly discovered Selby coalfield, the Selby Diversion was opened in 1983 as part of the East Coast Main Line running from Temple Hirst Junction, about 5 miles south of Selby, to Colton Junction, about 6 miles south of York. On this section of line, near Burn, with Drax Power Station in the distance, GNER Class 91 electric No. 91007 is speeding north with the 11.30 Kings Cross–Newcastle on Tuesday 28 January 1997. GNER was formed after privatisation of the railways in 1996, and No. 91007 is in its original GNER blue livery with red body stripe and gold lettering.

The Brush Class 60s were introduced as heavy freight locomotives in 1990 after sectorisation of UK railways and separation of passenger and freight operations. On Wednesday 22 January 1992 No. 60054 *Charles Babbage* is passing the lime and chalk quarry of Singleton Birch Ltd at Melton Ross heading the heavy 10.52 Lindsey–Leeds oil.

On Friday 6 May 1988 pairs of Class 37s were working the ore trains between the iron ore terminal at Immingham and the steelworks at Scunthorpe. No. 37002 in red stripe livery and with blanked out split headcode boxes and nose end doors is piloting No. 37225 in rail blue on a loaded ore train at Wrawby Junction, Barnetby.

During 1994, just before privatisation of the rail industry, LoadHaul, Transrail Freight and Mainline Freight were formed and the Class 60s were split between the three operators. Looking very smart in its LoadHaul black livery, No. 60038 is taking the Doncaster line at Wrawby Junction on Wednesday 2 October 1996 with a train from the Tioxide Works at Grimsby.

Sporting its special British Steel blue livery, which had been applied in July 1997, No. 60006 *Scunthorpe Ironmaster* is passing Wrawby Junction on empties heading back to Immingham on Saturday 16 August 1997. The large mechanical signal box of Great Central Railway design can be seen in the distance.

The lines to Doncaster, Gainsborough and Lincoln were controlled at Wrawby Junction with its fine array of semaphore signals. Not surprisingly it was a very popular spot for photography, and on Tuesday 29 October 1996 Class 60 No. 60064 *Black Tor* is restarting its ore train for Scunthorpe having been held on the relief line for a passenger train. LoadHaul bodyside branding has been applied on the triple grey body colours in lieu of complete repainting.

As part of the privatisation of BR, Freightliner Ltd was formed and in 1999 established its Heavy Haul business acquiring numerous Class 66 locomotives from General Motors in Canada. On Saturday 1 September 2001 Freightliner Heavy Haul Class 66/5 No. 66520 is passing Scunthorpe with empty coal hoppers from Immingham having taken a load for export. Class 56 No. 56038 in EWS colours is awaiting departure from the sidings with empty ore hoppers.

One of the thirty Romanian-built Class 56s, No. 56020 in standard British Rail blue livery is approaching the station at Stainforth & Hatfield on Thursday 17 March 1988 heading empty MGR hoppers from Scunthorpe. Hatfield Colliery, which closed in 2015, is in the background.

Class 56 No. 56047 was built at British Rail Engineering Ltd at Doncaster in 1978, and out of a total of 135 Class 56s was one of ninety painted in Railfreight Trainload grey livery with coal sector bodyside branding. It was withdrawn from Immingham in May 1999, but on Tuesday 7 February 1989 is passing Hatfield Colliery and approaching Thorne Junction with an MGR to Scunthorpe.

Throughout the years Doncaster has been a popular spot for photographers with the busy lines running virtually north/south through the station and with several road overbridges. The full Deltic timetable was introduced in June 1962 after the last Deltics had been delivered, and on 14 May 1963 No. D9016, named *Gordon Highlander* in July 1964, is leaving Doncaster with the Down 'White Rose'.

A variety of motive power could be seen at Doncaster, but one of the more unusual visitors was No. D6575, a Birmingham Railway Carriage & Wagon Co. Ltd Type 3 from the Southern Region whilst it was shedded at Hither Green, later to become Class 33. It is passing through the station on 14 May 1963 heading bulk cement empties from Uddingston in Scotland to Cliffe in Kent, having come on the train at York.

In the late afternoon of Wednesday 24 May 1978, Deltic No. 55005 *The Prince of Wales's Own Regiment of Yorkshire,* one of six Deltics initially allocated to Gateshead and all having regimental names, is slowing for its stop at Doncaster with the 16.08 Kings Cross–York. These 'York stoppers' were very tightly timed and enabled a Deltic to be used to its full potential. It is approaching Bridge Junction and Doncaster shed is in the background.

An afternoon departure from Doncaster on Wednesday 24 May 1978. No. 55018 *Ballymoss*, one of eight Deltics initially allocated to Finsbury Park and all named after racehorses, is accelerating the 15.40 Leeds–Kings Cross past Bridge Junction. The spire of St James' Church is dominant on the right, beyond which is Doncaster Minster.

The main reason to go to Doncaster at this time was to photograph Deltics, but a few InterCity HSTs had already started to appear on some of the East Coast expresses. Also on Wednesday 24 May 1978 power cars Nos 254010 and 254003 are working the Down 'Talisman' to Edinburgh, before the HSTs were fitted with deflector plates to the roof above the cab.

An afternoon departure from Doncaster seen from Hexthorpe Road bridge on Wednesday 25 May 1977. Deltic No. 55004 *Queen's Own Highlander,* one of eight initially allocated to Haymarket all with regimental names, is snaking away from the platform with the 13.00 Edinburgh–Kings Cross.

A morning departure from Doncaster seen from Hexthorpe Road bridge on Tuesday 30 May 1978. Deltic No. 55018 *Ballymoss* is heading the 07.05 Edinburgh–Kings Cross and in the background standing outside the 'Plant' is a Class 56 and a Class 50, with a Class 37 in the distance.

Sporting its new large logo blue livery, Class 56 No. 56116 has just crossed the River Don and is approaching Marshgate Junction shortly after passing Doncaster heading an MGR from Belmont Yard to Thorpe Marsh Power Station on Tuesday 12 April 1983. Doncaster Minster stands out clearly on the left.

Passing a fine array of semaphore signals adjacent to the NER signal box at Castleford on Tuesday 16 February 1988, Class 47/0 No. 47233 is heading the 06.56 Stanlow–Jarrow oil tanks. Built in 1965 and originally No. D1910, No. 47233 was withdrawn from Immingham in 1991 and subsequently cut up.

On Thursday 15 May 1980 in the late afternoon, Class 31/1 No. 31120 is passing the signal box at Goose Hill Junction, Normanton, with a weed-killing train heading back to Healey Mills. This fine Midland Railway signal box controlled the line to Wakefield Kirkgate and the original Midland main line from Leeds to Sheffield, but when the section from here to Oakenshaw Junction closed in June 1987, the box closed shortly afterwards, in October 1988.

In clean BR blue, English Electric Class 40 No. 40185 is passing the site of the former steam shed at Normanton, which closed in December 1967. On Thursday 15 May 1980 it is heading a Leeds–Stanlow empty oil train, and the original four-character train reporting panel has been modified with two spots as marker lights.

Class 56 No. 56132 is approaching Goose Hill Junction at Normanton on Thursday 24 July 1986 with a Stanlow–Leeds oil train. It is approaching the junction on the line from Wakefield Kirkgate, and on the left is what was formerly part of the Midland main line between Leeds and Sheffield.

Superbly turned out as one would expect for Royal Train duties, Class 47/4 No. 47585 *County of Cambridgeshire* is passing Wakefield Westgate on the empty stock returning to Wolverton from a royal visit to Leeds on Thursday 3 July 1986.

Dominated by the cooling towers of Ferrybridge Power Station, on Thursday 12 August 1982 Class 31/1 No. 31316 has just crossed the River Aire and is passing Brotherton with the 08.30 Sheffield–Scarborough, the original four-character route indicator panel having been modified. Built in 1962, No. 31316 was fitted with electric train heating in 1984, becoming No. 31446. In 1990 it was allocated to the Civil Engineers Department as No. 31546 and was finally withdrawn from Tinsley in November 1995 and subsequently cut up.

Milford Junction saw a considerable amount of freight activity, particularly coal traffic from the nearby Gascoigne Wood mine to the Aire Valley power stations. However, in the late afternoon of Tuesday 6 July 1993, Class 60 No. 60080 *Kinder Scout* in its Trainload Freight Construction livery is snaking across to the Castleford line with the returning Tilcon empties from Hull to Rylstone.

A busy scene at Gascoigne Wood, one of the largest and most modern pits in the UK. On Wednesday 14 June 1995 National Power Class 59/2 No. 59204 is almost ready to leave on its loaded train to one of the Aire Valley power stations as Class 56 No. 56135 *Port of Tyne Authority* is pulling its MGR through the automated loader, and in the background LoadHaul Class 56 No. 56102 is just arriving with its empties.

Displaying the Railfreight Coal subsector livery with the black diamonds on the sides, Class 58 No. 58041 *Ratcliffe Power Station* is passing Burton Salmon on Tuesday 20 October 1992 with a southbound loaded MGR from Gascoigne Wood. No. 58041 was one of twelve Class 58s later to move to Spain for use on construction trains on a new high-speed line from Madrid and the French border.

A view of the east end of a very busy Healey Mills Yard taken on 13 March 1980 as Class 47/0 No. 47277 fitted with remote control equipment is leaving with a rake of empty eastbound coal hoppers. Healey Mills opened in 1963 and became a traction maintenance depot in 1966. Facilities at the site were progressively run down during the 1980s and it finally closed in 2012, the site now resembling a forest.

Towards the end of 1983 I worked from an office in Ossett for a few years, barely 1 mile from Healey Mills, so not surprisingly Healey Mills and surrounding areas got a lot of attention, particularly at lunchtimes, which produced a considerable amount of varied traffic. On Wednesday 4 April 1984 Class 40 No. 40056 is preparing to leave on a Stanlow–Leeds oil train after a crew change. On the right is Class 47/0 No. 47196, which has just arrived on another eastbound oil train, with Class 56 No. 56098 on empty HAA wagons flanked by two Class 31/1s, Nos 31215 and 31240.

Overlooked by St Mary's Church at Horbury, a pair of Class 31/1s are passing the site of Horbury Millfield Road station, which had an island platform and which closed in November 1961. They are heading the Preston Docks–Lindsey oil empties towards Horbury Junction on Tuesday 21 February 1989 with No. 31319 in Railfreight large logo grey and No. 31212 in BR blue.

Following some overnight snow, on Monday 7 January 1985 Class 40 No. 40192 is powering a Stanlow–Leeds oil train past Horbury Junction where the Calder Valley line is joined by the line from Barnsley, almost 3 miles from Wakefield Kirkgate.

On Wednesday 26 April 1989, in smart large logo blue livery, Class 56 No. 56117 is passing the site of Horbury and Ossett station, which closed in 1970. The station had an island platform, hence the distance between the Up and Down running lines. Class 56 No. 56117 is heading the Cawoods container train of household coal from Blyth to Ellesmere Port.

Electric train heat fitted Class 37/4 No. 37425 *Sir Robert McAlpine/Concrete Bob* is passing through Horbury Cutting between Healey Mills and Horbury Junction on Wednesday 17 May 1989. Looking splendid in its large logo blue livery, it is heading the Dewsbury–Earles empty cement.

After some overnight snow, on Monday 23 January 1984 Class 40 No. 40195 has just left Healey Mills after a crew change and is approaching Horbury Cutting with a Stanlow–Leeds oil train.

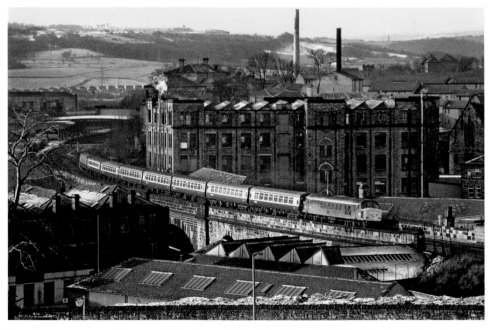

Dewsbury was generally regarded as the capital of the Heavy Woollen District of the then West Riding of Yorkshire. On Tuesday 17 February 1987 Peak Class 45/1 No. 45121 is restarting the 08.03 Liverpool–Newcastle away from its stop at Dewsbury Wellington Road.

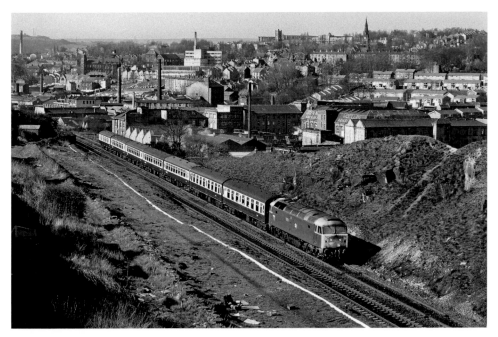

Class 47/4 No. 47407 *Aycliffe*, with its modified blue livery incorporating extended yellow above the cab, is climbing from Dewsbury towards Batley heading the 08.05 Liverpool–Newcastle on Wednesday 24 April 1985.

Hauling a smart rake of Regional Railways Trans-Pennine liveried coaches, Class 47/4 No. 47443 *North Eastern* is approaching Morley Tunnel with the 09.01 Liverpool–Newcastle on Wednesday 10 May 1989.

On Tuesday 24 July 1984 Peak Class 45/1 No. 45144 *Royal Signals* has just passed Batley with the 07.50 Scarborough–Liverpool. On the right is the track bed and the viaduct of the ex-GNR line from Wakefield to Bradford via Ossett and Dudley Hill, which closed in 1964, and the viaduct was demolished in the late 1980s.

Class 40s were regular power on the Stanlow–Leeds oil trains at this period, and on Tuesday 17 July 1984 Class 40 No. 40091 is heading towards Healey Mills on the Calder Valley main line near Thornhill with a loaded train from Stanlow. Thornhill Power Station is in the background, the coal-fired steam station of which was decommissioned in 1982 and subsequently demolished, including the cooling towers.

On Wednesday 28 November 1984 the Preston Docks–Lindsey oil empties is passing the site of Thornhill station, which closed in January 1962. It is being hauled by Class 56 No. 56117 and in the distance the main line to Leeds can be seen with a bridge over the River Calder.

By the summer of 1962 Deltics were a regular sight at Leeds Central, particularly on the Pullmans. On 1 July 1962 immaculate No. D9001 *St Paddy*, complete with silver buffers, is climbing away from Leeds Central with the Up 'Harrogate Sunday Pullman'. Introduced in February 1961, in July 1962 *St Paddy* had only just been named, was withdrawn from Finsbury Park in January 1980 and cut up shortly afterwards at BREL Doncaster.

Unusual motive power for the Up 'Yorkshire Pullman' on Tuesday 5 March 1963. Peak No. D183 is leaving the rather undistinguished and cramped terminus at Leeds Central (which I loved) with the Up 'Yorkshire Pullman'. D183 was one of fifty-six of the later Peaks built with Brush electrical equipment which later became Class 46, and No. D183 became No. 46046 in February 1974 under the TOPS renumbering scheme.

Leeds City, later named simply Leeds, was a much larger station than Leeds Central, and on 2 September 1979 steam heat Class 45/0 No. 45056 is leaving the east end of the station heading for the carriage sidings at Neville Hill with empty stock from an earlier arrival. The station, which had been rebuilt in 1967, is overlooked by the large City House office block, and in 2002 was further rebuilt and enlarged.

ScotRail InterCity-liveried Class 47/4 No. 47469 *Glasgow Chamber of Commerce* of Inverness is a long way from home on Thursday 30 October 1986 as it passes Marsh Lane on the way out of Leeds on the notorious double track bottleneck heading the 08.17 Holyhead–Newcastle.

In 1983 the pioneer English Electric Class 40 No. 40122, built as No. D200 in March 1958, was restored at Toton to full as built BR green livery, but with full yellow ends. On Wednesday 6 March 1985 No. D200 (40122) is coming out of Marsh Lane Cutting as it nears Neville Hill with the empty stock off the 10.40 Carlisle–Leeds.

The Leeds skyline has changed considerably since this photograph was taken on Good Friday 4 April 1980. Peak Class 46 No. 46053 is leaving Leeds with the 09.35 Carlisle–Nottingham, which has just reversed at the station.

In years gone by there was a junction at Beeston with a little used GN branch to a goods depot at Hunslet West. Deltic No. 55018 *Ballymoss* is heading the 17.30 Leeds–Kings Cross as it speeds towards its first stop at Wakefield Westgate, and the overgrown remains of the branch can be seen going off on the right.

On Tuesday 10 May 1977 Deltic No. 55012 *Crepello* is racing past Lofthouse Colliery as it nears Wakefield with the 17.30 Leeds–Kings Cross. On 21 March 1973 there was a bad accident at the colliery when some of the workings flooded resulting in the tragic death of seven miners. The colliery was finally closed in 1981 and the site has now been attractively landscaped. *Crepello* had been given its TOPS number in February 1974, and was withdrawn from Finsbury Park in May 1981 and subsequently cut up.

After about fifteen years of high-speed haulage by the Deltics, HSTs took over some of the services from May 1979 and in the late 1980s the East Coast Main Line services to Leeds were electrified. Somewhat unusually, Rail Express-liveried Class 90 No. 90016 is heading the 15.05 Kings Cross–Leeds on Friday 14 August 1982, presumably deputising for a Class 91 electric. It is on the outskirts of Leeds passing the site of Beeston station, which closed in 1953.

On Wednesday 20 June 1990 Hunslet Barclay Class 20/9s Nos 20905 *Iona* and 20902 *Lorna* are crossing the thirty-two-arch, 476-yard-long Lockwood Viaduct on the way from Huddersfield to Penistone with the weed-killing train on its journey round parts of West and South Yorkshire. There were 228 of these English Electric Type 1 diesels first introduced in 1957 and large numbers have survived. Class 20/9s Nos 20905 and 20902 were two of six modified from the original Class 20/0s and sold to Hunslet Barclay in 1989 for work on weed-killing trains.

In work-stained BR blue, Class 37/0 No. 37165 is crossing the River Calder at Mirfield on Wednesday 28 October 1981 heading for Healey Mills on a train of four-wheeled oil tanks. The viaduct on the far right is on the closed L&NWR New Line from Heaton Lodge Junction to Leeds.

In smart-looking clean Railfreight red stripe livery, Class 47/3 No. 47301 of Thornaby is passing Mirfield on Thursday 11 February 1988 with the 10.45 Weaste–Port Clarence train of 100-ton bogie tanks.

After overnight snow followed by morning sunshine on Wednesday 25 January 1984, I quickly rearranged some survey appointments to take advantage of the Christmas card conditions. Near Mirfield over a dozen loco-hauled trains were seen in about two hours with motive power including Class 37s, 47s, Peaks and a Class 40. Class 37/0 No. 37071 is passing the site of the old steam shed heading west with a freight which had been stabled overnight at Healey Mills.

In very different conditions on Tuesday 9 May 1989, Class 56 No. 56133 *Crewe Locomotive Works* is heading west along the Calder Valley near Mirfield with the Cawoods container train of household coal from Blyth to Ellesmere Port.

Peak Class 45/0 No. 45014 *The Cheshire Regiment* is passing the site of a once busy marshalling yard at Brighouse heading the summer Saturday 13.53 Blackpool–Sheffield on 5 September 1981. Not surprisingly some of the large Victorian mill premises in Brighouse have now been converted to form desirable residential flats.

The summer Saturday 07.57 Weymouth–Bradford Interchange is passing the small signal box at Elland in the Calder Valley behind Peak Class 45/0 No. 45003 on 12 September 1981. Although Elland station closed in September 1962, part of the large goods warehouse can still be seen on the right.

Work-stained Peak Class 45/0 No. 45023 *The Royal Pioneer Corps* is leaving Halifax on Easter Monday 12 April 1982 with a return footex to Sheffield, Halifax Town having lost 5-1 to Sheffield United.

During summer 1979 the Calder Valley line was often used as a diversionary route on Sundays due to engineering work on the Standedge route. 16 September was one such day and Class 47/4 No. 47401 is passing Sowerby Bridge with the diverted 09.55 Newcastle–Liverpool. It is passing the site of the steam shed and the former stone-built water tower and coaling stage is to the left of No. 47401, now reroofed and used as a garage service bay. Wainhouse Tower, a famous local landmark, can be seen on the horizon.

The diverted 08.40 Liverpool–Newcastle is approaching Horsfall Tunnel in the Calder Valley on Sunday 16 September 1979 headed by Class 46 No. 46046. It is about 3 miles from Hebden Bridge and will rejoin the Standedge route at Heaton Lodge Junction, Mirfield.

An unidentified Class 25 has just emerged from Horsfall Tunnel, in the distance, on Sunday 16 September heading the Hull–Red Bank empty newspaper vans.

At Gauxholme, almost 1 mile west of Todmorden, the railway crosses the Rochdale Canal twice. On Sunday 23 September 1979 the diverted 12.20 Newcastle–Liverpool is crossing the Rochdale Canal on Gauxholme No. 1 Viaduct behind Class 47/0 No. 47088. Just beyond the rear of the train is Gauxholme No. 2 Viaduct, which also crosses the Rochdale Canal and incorporates four stone castellated towers at the ends of a cast-iron span.

Just east of Todmorden the line to Burnley branches off the Calder Valley main line at Hall Royd Junction and then climbs at mainly 1 in 65 for about 5 miles to Copy Pit Summit. On Easter Monday 12 April 1982 Class 47/4 No. 47464 comes cautiously downgrade round a sharp corner near Cornholme on a Blackpool–York excursion.

On Saturday 9 April 1983 Class 47/0 No. 47165 is on the climb to Copy Pit heading a Leeds–Burnley footex. It is crossing Lydgate Viaduct on the 1 in 65 gradient, having just emerged from Kitson Wood Tunnel. The away supporters would return home pleased after a 2-1 victory.

The transition from steam in the late 1960s led to many diesel and steam combinations, and in June 1967 the 15.05 from Bradford Interchange to Kings Cross was hauled between Bradford and Leeds by Sulzer Class 2 No. D5100 (later Class 24/1 No. 24100) and a Fairburn 2-6-4T. This was a regular working at the time used to train crews on the new diesels. The pair are passing the remains of St Dunstan's station, which had closed in September 1952, but the signal box remained at the junction of lines leading to the carriage sidings and also the ex-GNR line to Keighley and Halifax via Queensbury from which passenger services had been withdrawn in 1955. Above the rear coach is Mill Lane signal box on the ex-L&YR main line to Halifax.

Nicely turned out Class 47/4 No. 47541 is climbing steeply out of Bradford towards Laisterdyke with the lunchtime express from Bradford Interchange to Kings Cross in January 1975. The entrance to Hammerton Street depot is on the left in the distance.

By the late 1970s Deltics were regular visitors to Bradford Interchange and could sometimes be seen on the lunchtime express to Kings Cross and also on the early evening express to Kings Cross. On Tuesday 24 April 1979 I was working in Bradford and left the office to see No. 55018 *Ballymoss* leaving Bradford Interchange on the 17.30 to Kings Cross, making a spectacular departure working on just one engine.

At a time when Bradford Interchange generated a considerable amount of parcels traffic, on Tuesday 10 July 1990, InterCity-liveried Class 47/4 No. 47568 *Royal Engineers Postal & Courier Services* is approaching Mill Lane Junction, having just left Bradford Interchange with the 19.42 parcels to Leeds.

The Saturday lunchtime empty newspaper vans from Bradford Forster Square to Manchester Red Bank produced a variety of motive power, but a Class 25 on such a big train was unusual. On 25 October 1980, Class 25/2 No. 25099 is leaving Forster Square station a few years before the large original MR station, goods warehouse and Valley Road goods depot were all swept away and most of the site redeveloped, the new modern station being a shadow of its former self.

On Thursday 22 April 1982 Class 25/2 No. 25145 is leaving Bradford Valley Road goods and approaching Manningham Junction with a short pick up goods returning to Healey Mills. The land behind the train is now part of a huge retail park.

Following electrification of the main line to Leeds from Kings Cross in 1988, the connection to Bradford Forster Square via Shipley was not electrified for another few years. As a result electrically hauled trains from Kings Cross to Forster Square, sometimes complete with the electric locomotive on one end and the DVT on the other, were dragged by diesels from Leeds. On Monday 4 June 1990 Class 47/4 No. 47407 is hauling the 15.50 Kings Cross–Bradford Forster Square away from its stop at Shipley attached to DVT No. 82205, the electric loco having been detached at Leeds.

On Saturday 16 November 1974 Peak No. 58 *The King's Own Royal Border Regiment* (later Class 45/0 No. 45043) has just passed Shipley Leeds Junction and is approaching Shipley Bingley Junction with the Down 'Thames-Clyde Express'. After steam had finished on BR, it was decided that the 'D' and 'E' prefix to modern traction numbers should be removed, and No. 58 was given its TOPS number in 1975. No. 58 is in the new BR standard blue livery, with full yellow ends including the four-character headcode display, and is passing where platforms were constructed on this side of the triangle during the mid-1980s.

Class 47/4 No. 47594 is approaching Shipley on Good Friday 24 March 1978 heading the 09.35 Carlisle–Nottingham. Prominent in the background is Salts Mill, built in 1853 by Sir Titus Salt, and now part of the UNESCO World Heritage site at Saltaire.

In the early 1980s pairs of Class 31s were the regular power for the Tilcon stone trains from Rylstone on the Grassington branch to Hull. On Tuesday 14 June 1983 Class 31/1s Nos 31163 and 31220 have just passed Guiseley Junction at Shipley with the 10.18 Rylstone–Hull Tilcon. In 1984 No. 31220 was fitted with electric train heating and renumbered 31441. One of the four tracks on this section of line has already been lifted and work is in hand to remove a second which has not been used for several years.

The Down 'Thames-Clyde Express' is near Gargrave on Saturday 7 March 1970 hauled by Peak Class 45/0 No. 60 *Lytham St Annes*. Originally numbered D60 when it was introduced in 1962, it was to receive its TOPS No. 45022 in November 1974.

Class 40 No. 40025 is accelerating the 15.51 Nottingham–Carlisle away from its stop at Keighley on Saturday 4 August 1979 as a DMU prepares to run into the station to commence its journey to Leeds.

A smart looking large logo blue Class 47/4 No. 47479 with white painted roof is leaving Skipton on bank holiday Monday 4 May 1987 with the 07.40 Hull–Carlisle. The former steam shed is on the right and it is passing the site of Skipton North Junction where the line to Earby and Colne, which closed in 1970, left the main line.

Class 31/1s Nos 31124 and 31226 are nearing their destination at the Rylstone quarry on the single line of the branch from Embsay Junction at Skipton, which originally went to the terminus at Grassington & Threshfield. They are heading the empty four-wheeled Tilcon hoppers from Hull on Saturday 30 April 1983.

Between Christmas and New Year, the morning of Thursday 27 December 1984 produced a dusting of snow on the ground in the Yorkshire Dales. Class 31/4 No. 31402 has just passed the long since closed station at Bell Busk with the Leeds–Carlisle train, just before a steam special was due on its way from Leeds to Appleby.

The 11.00 Barrow–Euston is restarting from its stop at Grange-over-Sands on bank holiday Monday 5 May 1980 hauled by Class 47/4 No. 47445. It is hard to believe that the sands adjacent to the promenade in this picture are now completely grassed over.

The fisherman seems oblivious to the Derby Class 116 two-car diesel multiple unit leaving Ravenglass on a service from Carnforth to Carlisle via the Cumbrian coast on Monday 25 August 1980. It is crossing the River Mite and some of the mountains of the Lake District can be seen in the far distance.

Snow-covered Ingleborough dominates the background as Peak Class 45/0 No. 45004 *Royal Irish Fusilier* passes Kettlesbeck Bridge, between Clapham and Eldroth, heading the Heysham Moss–ICI Haverton Hill four-wheel empty anhydrous ammonia tanks on Saturday 12 December 1981.

The best-known structure on the magnificent Settle and Carlisle line is Batty Moss Viaduct at Ribblehead, generally known simply as Ribblehead Viaduct. It has twenty-four arches, is 440 yards long and 104 feet high at its highest point. On Saturday 30 August 1997 English Welsh & Scottish Railways (EWS) Class 60 No. 60004 is coming off the viaduct with empty gypsum hoppers from Kirkby Thore.

The tallest viaduct on the Settle and Carlisle line is Smardale at 131 feet above Scandal Beck and the track bed of the ex-NER line between Tebay and Darlington, which closed in 1962. It has twelve arches and is 237 yards long. On Saturday 11 March 1989 Class 47/4 No. 47608 is crossing on the 1 in 100 downgrade section between Kirkby Stephen and Appleby heading the diverted 10.30 Euston–Glasgow.

Arten Gill Viaduct has eleven arches, is 220 yards long and 117 feet above Artengill Beck. After an early start from home on Tuesday 27 April 1982, and a brisk walk up the hillside, Class 40 No. 40079 came trundling downhill from Dent, in the far distance, heading the 06.00 Carlisle–Bescot freight, which includes a nuclear flask.

On Saturday 28 April 1984 Peak Class 45/1 No. 45107 is crossing Dent Head Viaduct with the 09.07 Leeds–Carlisle, having just emerged from Blea Moor Tunnel, which is in the distance. Dent Head Viaduct has ten arches, is 596 feet long and 100 feet high. It is adjacent to the road leading to Dent village, which is almost 5 miles away.

Saturday 18 May 1996 saw the return of a coal train to the Settle and Carlisle line. In the late afternoon a pair of Class 37/0s, Nos 37026 *Shap Fell* and 37116 *Sister Dora*, are passing Settle Junction with a Milford Sidings–Carlisle British Fuel containerised coal train, which would then be forwarded to Scottish distribution depots. No. 37026 is in faded Speedlink Distribution sector markings and was withdrawn within the week. No. 37116 is in BR blue, but with Transrail 'T' logo and name on the sides.

With the unmistakable flat top of Ingleborough in the background, the celebrity Class 40 No. D200 (40122) is passing Blea Moor with the 16.00 Leeds–Carlisle on Saturday 6 August 1983.

Passing Dent, the highest station in England at an altitude of 1,150 feet above sea level, Class 40 No. 40172 is heading a special Hunslet–Carlisle freight on Sunday 13 May 1979. The snow fences formed of sleepers and erected to protect the line from drifting snow in winter are in a dilapidated condition, and Dent Head Viaduct can just be seen in the far distance. Dent village is almost 5 miles from the station and 400 feet lower.

On Wednesday 4 November 1981 Class 25/2s Nos 25215 and 25123 have just crossed Dandry Mire Viaduct and are passing Garsdale heading a Carlisle–Tinsley freight formed mainly of four-wheel vacuum braked vans. Garsdale was originally named Hawes Junction where the branch to Hawes left the mainline. The branch closed in 1959, but part of the track bed can be seen at the bottom of the picture.

Beneath the shadow of Wild Boar Fell, Class 60 No. 60012 is approaching Ais Gill Summit, highest point on the Settle and Carlisle line at 1,169 feet above sea level. On Saturday 13 March 1999 it is heading a southbound loaded Merry-go-Round coal train of HAA four-wheel wagons, thought to be from Hunterston to Milford Junction. No. 60012 is lettered EW&S in the corporate maroon and gold livery, which was introduced after the three Trainload Freight companies had been sold to US operator Wisconsin Central in 1996. EW&S later shortened to EWS.

Class 40 No. 40184 is climbing steadily up the 1 in 100 from Kirkby Stephen towards Birkett Tunnel on Wednesday 2 September 1981 heading the 12.20 Carlisle–Severn Tunnel Junction with a mixed load which appears to include some china-clay empties for St Blazey, sheeted steel carriers for South Wales and a nuclear flask for Hinkley Point.

An unusual sight on the Settle and Carlisle line was a locomotive in Network SouthEast livery, but on Saturday 23 April 1988 Class 47/4 No. 47583 *County of Hertfordshire* has just crossed Smardale Viaduct and is heading towards its next stop at Kirkby Stephen on the 12.37 Carlisle–Leeds.

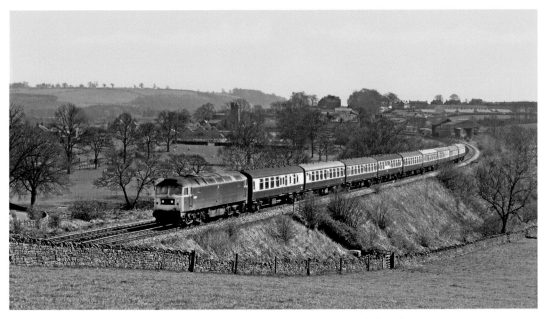

In the Eden Valley, on the easier grades between Appleby and Carlisle, Class 47/4 No. 47535 is accelerating the Saturday 09.40 Leicester–Glasgow away from Lazonby and Kirkoswald, about 15 miles from Carlisle.

Peaks will always be associated with passenger trains on the Settle and Carlisle line from their introduction in the early 1960s, and high above the River Eden, just south of Baron Wood Tunnels, Class 45/0 No. 45024 is heading south with the 11.50 Glasgow–Nottingham on Saturday 26 April 1980.

On Saturday 13 April 1963, with the station clock showing 3.10 p.m., the Down 'Royal Scot' prepares to leave Carlisle behind English Electric Type 4 No. D373, being admired by a group of spotters. Having been built by English Electric at Vulcan Foundry in January 1962 and allocated to Camden, in March 1974 it was given its TOPS No. 40173 and was withdrawn in August 1981 from Haymarket.

At 3.55 p.m., Peak No. D30 is arriving at platform 3 at Carlisle heading the Down 'Waverley', seemingly a very busy train on Saturday 13 April 1963. In the distance on the opposite platform an English Electric Type 4 is reversing onto an Up express. No. D30 was built in May 1961 at Derby Works and initially allocated to Derby. It was given its TOPS No. 45029 in April 1975 and was withdrawn from Tinsley in July 1987.

On Tuesday 23 May 1961 the eight-coach Up 'Caledonian', which left Glasgow Central at 8.30 a.m. on its run to London Euston, is entering the Lune Gorge, just south of Tebay. Motive power is provided by English Electric Type 4 No. D297, which later became Class 40 No. 40097 under the TOPS renumbering system. It is displaying express headcode white discs, which were later replaced by a central headcode panel.

Good Friday 12 April 1963 was a day of blustery showers on the Cumbrian Fells, but in a welcome patch of sun English Electric Type 4 No. D383 storms past Greenholme on the climb to Shap Summit with the Down 'Royal Scot' when the English Electric Type 4s were starting to monopolise the Anglo-Scottish expresses on the West Coast Main Line. No. D383 has the original small yellow warning ends, was renumbered 40183 in March 1974 and was withdrawn in June 1983.

In rather work-stained original two-tone green livery, but with full yellow ends, Brush Type 4 No. D1950, becoming Class 47/0 No. 47259 in March 1974 under the TOPS renumbering system, is passing Bessygill on the climb to Shap Summit with an Up express in October 1967.

Prior to full electrification of the West Coast Main Line in 1974, from the late 1960s extra power was needed for the principal Anglo-Scottish expresses to relieve the English Electric Type 4s, and so appeared the English Electric Class 50s, as they soon became known. The trains were often worked by pairs of Class 50s, but on Sunday 29 June 1969 No. D432 was working solo past Greenholme on the climb to Shap Summit with a Down express. No. D432 was renumbered 50032 under the TOPS scheme, named *Courageous* in July 1978 and, in common with other Class 50s, ended its days working from both Paddington and Waterloo to the south-west. It was withdrawn from Laira in October 1990, but was not one of about eighteen Class 50s that eluded the cutter's torch.

On Friday 13 March 1970 a fully loaded-up train of car flats is drifting down Shap at Greenholme behind Brush Type 4 No. 1712, which is in BR blue but with its pre-TOPS number of 47123, which it received in March 1974. In the distance work can be seen on the M6 motorway, which was to open later in 1970.

The West Coast Main Line in Cumbria is extremely scenic, particularly the section through the Lune Gorge where a pair of Class 86/4s are seen heading north, with the River Lune visible at a lower level. Nos 86410 and 86437 are both in the 'main line' livery, which was later developed into the InterCity swallow scheme, and are heading the 13.10 Dee Marsh–Mossend empty steel flats on Saturday 14 May 1988.

With the majestic snow-dusted Howgills as a backdrop, Class 47/3 No. 47332 is passing Docker on Saturday 19 March 1994 heading a Mossend–Warrington freight. It is in the Civil Engineers 'Dutch' yellow and grey livery, but in 1999 was rebuilt as Class 57/0 No. 57007.

In 1992 three Class 90s were given European railway liveries as part of the Freightconnection Exhibition in Birmingham. No. 90129 was painted in German DB red livery and named *Frachtverbindungen*, complete with Crewe depot eagle logo on the cab side. On Tuesday 10 August 1993 it has just passed Winwick Junction north of Warrington with an Up freight.

On Friday 26 March 1993 Class 90 No. 90021 is approaching Acton Grange Junction, south of Warrington, having just crossed the Manchester Ship Canal. It is heading an Up mail train and is in Railfreight Distribution livery with a cast double-arrow logo beneath the cab window.

Class 47/3 No. 47363 has just left the West Coast Main Line at Acton Grange Junction on Tuesday 28 May 1985. It is hauling a mixed freight including some specialist top-discharge tanks used for carrying highly toxic material. It is on the way to Ellesmere Port, and the electrified main line can be seen in the background, beyond which is Warrington.

Class 25/2 No. 25200 and Class 25/1 No. 25051 are approaching Arpley Junction with a Widnes–Earles empty cement train, having just passed beneath Warrington Bank Quay station on the main line on Wednesday 29 May 1985. Like many of the fleet of Class 25s, No. 25200 is fitted with a three-piece miniature snowplough.

The English Electric Type 1, later Class 20, was introduced in 1957 and eventually 228 were built up to 1968. They proved to be very successful and could be seen virtually all over the BR system on a variety of mainly freight duties. They were regularly to be seen working in pairs, and on Tuesday 28 May 1985 Nos 20049 and 20180 are passing the Lever Bros complex at Warrington, near Monks Siding, with a Merry-go-Round coal train for Fiddlers Ferry Power Station.

An unidentified Class 37 has just passed Frodsham and is crossing the River Weaver with a train of loaded ballast wagons from Penmaenmawr for the Manchester area on Wednesday 29 March 1995.

On Saturday 18 April 1981 Class 47/4 No. 47523 is leaving Chester with a Holyhead–Euston train as a DMU also leaves on a Manchester service. The scene is dominated by the imposing ex-L&NWR Chester No. 2 signal box, the largest in Chester, which controlled the east end of the station and the lines to Manchester and Crewe. It was demolished about 1984 after being replaced by a new power box.

Southport sees very little freight activity these days, but on Monday 12 May 1980 Class 25/2 No. 25119, fitted with a miniature snow plough, is leaving the yard heading for Wigan with a rake of empty house coal wagons and one low-profile van.

Emerging from the cavernous approach to Liverpool Lime Street, Class 31/4 No. 31465 in its smart Regional Railways livery is arriving with the 12.30 from Manchester Victoria on Saturday 24 April 1993. When the UK railways were sectorised in 1982, the majority of the Class 31s were allocated to the freight business, but some operated Regional Railways services, mainly allocated to Crewe Diesel Depot. No. 31465 appeared in 1960 as No. D5637, was renumbered 31213 in 1974, was converted to ETH operation in 1985 and renumbered 31465.

Following the introduction of HSTs on ECML services in 1978, Deltics soon found work on Trans-Pennine services from Newcastle and York to Liverpool. Towards the end of their distinguished careers, on Sunday 20 December 1981, No. 55022 *Royal Scots Grey* is preparing to leave Lime Street on 1E22, the 19.10 Liverpool–York with an appropriate headboard depicting the imminent end of the magnificent Deltics. After this trip *Royal Scots Grey* only worked two more service trains, and on 2 January 1982 it worked the final BR Deltic powered train, 1F50, the 14.32 Edinburgh Waverley–Kings Cross. Appropriately six Deltics out of a class of twenty-two have been preserved.

Peak Class 45/1 No. 45137 *The Bedfordshire and Hertfordshire Regiment (T.A.)* is nearing its destination with the 07.50 Scarborough–Liverpool on Tuesday 29 May 1984. It is passing through the impressive Olive Mount Cutting at Edge Hill, 80 feet deep, cut out of solid sandstone, opened in 1830 and widened to four tracks in 1871. The branch to Bootle diverging to the left is controlled by Olive Mount signal box in the distance.

The 17.14 Manchester Victoria–Blackpool North generally produced either a Class 31 or a Class 37 in Regional Railways livery. However, on Tuesday 22 June 1993 Class 37/4 No. 37408 *Loch Rannoch* appeared in its clean large logo blue livery complete with Scottish Region 'Scottie dog' emblem on the side. It is approaching its stop at Bolton with what appears to be a well-loaded train.

In the early 1990s Bolton parcels depot generated a considerable amount of traffic, particularly in the early evenings. On Wednesday 28 April 1993 Class 47/4 No. 47547 is passing Agecroft heading empty parcels vans to Bolton from Crewe. It is in rather faded Network SouthEast livery having been transferred to Crewe in July 1992 and had its *University of Oxford* nameplates removed.

Looking very smart in its InterCity livery with matching coaches, Class 47/8 No. 47823 *SS Great Britain* is heading the 12.45 Glasgow–Paddington on Tuesday 11 May 1993. It is passing what was Agecroft Junction, which gave access to the steam shed. In the distance is Agecroft Power Station, which closed early in 1993, was demolished in 1994 and is now the site of HM Prison Forest Bank. No. 47823 was renumbered 47787 in September 1994 and is now preserved as *Windsor Castle* by West Coast Railways.

Class 47/0 No. 47029 passing through Stockport station with British Oxygen Company tanks on bank holiday Monday 6 May 1985, probably running from the BOC depot at Ditton to Broughton Lane, Sheffield.

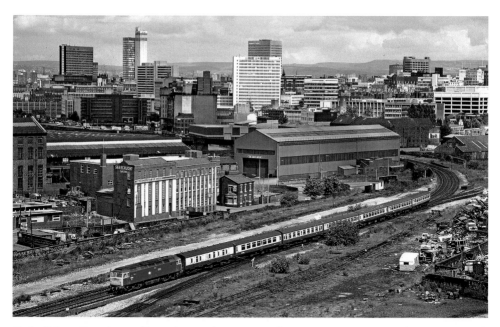

Ordsall Lane Junction on Saturday 3 July 1982 as Class 47/4 No. 47404 *Hadrian* passes with the 11.16 Newcastle–Liverpool having just left Manchester Victoria. The Manchester skyline has changed dramatically since this photograph was taken from Ordsall Lane flats, which have since been demolished and the site redeveloped.

In the 1990s, prior to privatisation, Class 37/4s were used on a number of what became known as the Manchester 'Club Train' workings, operating long-distance commuter traffic into and out of Manchester at peak times. One such working was the 17.14 Manchester Victoria–Blackpool North, which is approaching Salford Crescent on Tuesday 11 May 1993 behind Regional Railways No. 37422 *Robert F. Fairlie, Locomotive Engineer 1831–1885*, which had been repainted and named a few days earlier.

On Saturday 25 April 1992 Class 47/0 No. 47190 in Railfreight Petroleum livery is approaching Manchester Victoria with a neat-looking eastbound freight of boxcars. It is passing the site of Manchester Exchange, which closed to passengers in May 1969 when all remaining services were redirected to Manchester Victoria, although it remained operational for newspaper trains until the 1980s. Part of one platform can be seen and in the distance is the Threllfalls Brewery building, which is now the Deva City Office Park.

Peak Class 45/1 No. 45126 is coming cautiously down the 1 in 59 gradient from Miles Platting towards Manchester Victoria. It is heading the Sunday Leeds–Red Bank empty newspaper vans formed mainly of four-wheeled vans in Parcels Sector livery on 15 February 1987. It is passing Manchester Victoria East Junction where the line diverging to the left leads to Red Bank carriage sidings, along which the train will go after reversing at Victoria.

Regional Railways Class 37/4 No. 37429 *Eisteddfod Genedlaethol* is passing the site of Red Bank carriage sidings, which had been abandoned in 1990. It is heading for Newton Heath with empty stock from a morning Blackpool–Manchester Victoria 'Club Train' on Thursday 30 June 1994.

Sunset at Stalybridge on Saturday 31 January 1987. Class 47/4 No. 47426 is leaving with the 13.00 Bangor–York and starting the climb of about 7 miles to Diggle and the entrance to Standedge Tunnel.

Class 47/4 No. 47621 *Royal County of Berkshire* looks splendid in clean InterCity livery hauling a full rake of coaches in Regional Railways livery. On Tuesday 28 April 1987 it is heading the 13.00 Bangor–York near Midge Hill on the climb to Diggle. Introduced in April 1964 as No. D1728, it was withdrawn in 2013 as No. 47839 and broken up at Eastleigh.

The twenty-three-arch Saddleworth Viaduct, sometimes called Uppermill Viaduct, is just over 1 mile from Diggle on the falling gradient to Stalybridge, and crosses the Huddersfield Narrow Canal. On Monday 3 June 1985 Class 25/2s Nos 25209 and 25181 are crossing with Leeds–Stanlow empty oil tanks.

On Saturday 16 February 1991 Pathfinder Tours ran the 'Sulzer Salute Rail Tour', which originated at Swindon. Class 25/3 No. 25322, running with its original No. D7672 was named *Tamworth Castle* between April 1989 and April 1991, and was used on a circuitous route between Sheffield and Hellifield. In typical wintry Pennine conditions, in the early afternoon it is drifting downhill between Diggle and Saddleworth.

Class 37/0 No. 37124 is passing Marsden on Saturday 22 February 1986 heading a short train of four-wheel tanks from ICI Folly Lane at Runcorn to Seal Sands near Billingham. It has just emerged from the 3-mile-long Standedge Tunnel, out of sight round the corner, and is starting the long descent to Huddersfield and then to Mirfield in the Calder Valley.

Class 40 No. 40068 is passing Golcar on the climb to Standedge Tunnel on Monday 4 April 1983 heading the Heaton–Manchester Red Bank empty newspaper vans, a regular working for a Class 40 at this time. After the abolition of route indicators, many disc-fitted Class 40s were set to display two white discs as standard front display. Once four tracks on this section from Huddersfield, two had been removed a few years earlier.

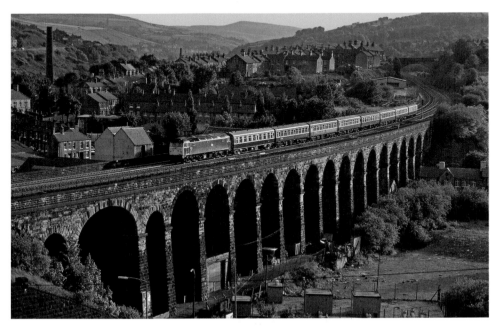

In the early evening of Tuesday 3 July 1984, Class 47/4 No. 47533 is crossing the impressive twenty-arch Longwood Viaduct at Milnsbridge with the 18.05 Liverpool–Newcastle, about 2 miles before its next stop at Huddersfield. Longwood Viaduct is the largest of four viaducts in the Colne Valley between Huddersfield and Marsden.

On Saturday 23 October 1982 Class 56 No. 56074 *Kellingley Colliery* has just emerged from Paddock Cutting after passing Huddersfield with a Healey Mills–Fiddlers Ferry Merry-go-Round coal train. No. 56074 was one of two Class 56s built with roof-mounted flashing beacons to indicate remote-control operation at some power station sites, but they were seldom used so were eventually removed.

Leaving the moorland of the Pennines behind and with Longwood Viaduct in the distance, Class 47/4 No. 47429 is nearing Huddersfield at Paddock heading the 12.05 Liverpool–York on 23 September 1979. Two of the original four tracks on this section of line out of Huddersfield were removed a few years earlier.

A morning southbound inter-regional train is accelerating away from its stop at York on Monday 1 September 1975 behind Peak Class 45/0 No. 45012.

Class 40 No. 40176 is passing Dringhouses Yard, almost 2 miles south of York station, with a freight bound for Healey Mills on Thursday 26 May 1977. This busy yard had been modernised in 1961 when it incorporated some hump shunting, but closed in 1987, after which the site was redeveloped as a large housing estate.

I doubt Class 25/3 No. 25320 had been diagrammed to work the seventeen-vehicle Heaton–Manchester Red Bank empty newspaper vans on Sunday 18 June 1978. A Class 40 was the usual power, so I suspect there had been a last-minute failure of the Class 40. No. 25320 has just passed Skelton Junction where the Harrogate line leaves the East Coast Main Line, and York Yard North is on the left.

An unusual sight at York on Tuesday 11 April 1978 was one of the ten original Peaks, which at the time didn't generally stray far from the Toton area. No. 44004 was built at Derby in September 1959, appearing as No. D4 and named *Great Gable*, but in this picture the nameplates have been removed. It is coming off the freight avoiding line at Holgate Junction, just south of York station, heading an Up coal train.

A meeting of Deltics on Sunday 26 September 1976 at Severus Curve, Clifton, not far from York station. No. 55022 *Royal Scots Grey* is slowing for its stop at York with the 10.00 Edinburgh Waverley–London Kings Cross as No. 55009 *Alycidon* accelerates away from its stop with the 10.00 London Kings Cross–Edinburgh.

On Thursday 26 May 1977 Class 37/0 No. 37127 is passing Holgate Sidings with a train of eight-wheel bogie oil tanks bound for Teesside. On the left are the remains of what was York Racecourse Platform, also known as York Holgate Excursion Platform, which was only used on race days, and was last used in 1939.

On the beautiful early evening of Sunday 18 June 1978, and with York Minster prominent in the background, Deltic No. 55013 *The Black Watch* is starting the 18.58 tightly timed service from York to Kings Cross formed of Mk1 stock.

Before the days of the Selby diversion when East Coast Main Line trains south from York travelled via Selby, Deltic No. 55002 *The Kings Own Yorkshire Light Infantry* is accelerating away from Chaloners Whin Junction on Sunday 12 October 1980 heading the 15.50 York–Kings Cross. The junction was about 2 miles south of York and the track bed here is now a footpath and cycleway.

A feature of the railway at Scarborough in 1985 was the impressive signal gantry and the NER-built Falsgrave signal box on the approach to the terminal station. The box controlled lines approaching the station and also the line that went off to Whitby, which closed in 1965. The NER-built signal box is now a Grade II listed building, and following decommissioning in 2010, the gantry was re-erected at Grosmont on the North Yorkshire Moors Railway. On Saturday 16 February 1985 Class 31/4 No. 31439 is leaving with the 11.53 to York.

No. 40004 was one of the first English Electric Type 4s to be built, appearing in May 1958 as No. D204 and initially allocated to Stratford on the Great Eastern section. It received its TOPS number, 40004, in March 1974 and was finally withdrawn from Longsight in September 1984 and cut up at Crewe in 1986. On Saturday 28 May 1977 it is racing past Pilmoor heading the 09.40 Great Yarmouth–Newcastle. The remains of the signal box can just be seen in the distance where the lines from Harrogate (closed in 1967) and Pickering (closed in 1953) joined the East Coast Main Line.

On Saturday 14 May 1977 Deltic No. 55018 *Ballymoss* is leaving the imposing NER station at Darlington with the 09.20 Newcastle–Kings Cross.

Industrial Teesside on Tuesday 23 February 1982, a scene which has now changed dramatically. Class 31/1 No. 31303 is approaching South Bank with a train of empties from the South Bank coke ovens, which are in full production in the background on the left. The huge Lackenby steelworks complex, which closed in 2015, is just out of sight on the right of this picture.

Between Grangetown and South Bank on 23 February 1982 as Class 31/1s Nos 31285 and 31201 are passing with a train of rolled steel from BSC Redcar.

For many years the North East was a stronghold for Class 37s working from Thornaby and Tyne on a variety of freight services. On Tuesday 27 July 1982 Class 37/0 No. 37082 is passing Hartlepool with an unfitted coal train from Horden Colliery, with Hartlepool Docks in the distance.

Looking towards South Bank from near Grangetown, Class 37/0 No. 37123 is passing the South Bank coke ovens with a train of empties heading for Redcar. Without doubt the Class 37s are one of the most successful designs ever to run on Britain's railways, introduced in 1960 and at home on either freight or passenger services throughout the UK. No. 37123 appeared in April 1963 as No. D6823 and was initially allocated to Cardiff Canton, but by 1966 had been moved to the North East. Not surprisingly numerous Class 37s have been preserved.

Running alongside the North Sea, about 2 miles north of Hartlepool, Class 37/0 No. 37082 is heading back to Horden Colliery with a train of empties from South Bank coke ovens. It has just passed Cemetery North Junction close to the large Steetley Chemical Works in the distance.

In its original two-tone green livery with small yellow warning panel, on Sunday 23 July 1967 Brush Type 4 No. D1986 has just crossed the King Edward Bridge as it leaves Newcastle with an Up car carrier. Built in January 1966, No. D1986 was renumbered 47284 in March 1974 and was withdrawn in November 1999.

On Wednesday 17 August 1977, Deltic No. 55002 *The King's Own Yorkshire Light Infantry* is accelerating hard away from King Edward Bridge Junction at Bensham as it leaves Newcastle heading the 08.30 Newcastle–Kings Cross.

A view from the castle keep at Newcastle overlooking the complicated track work where the line diverges to the left across High Level Bridge to Sunderland leaving the East Coast Main Line. Deltic No. 55004 *Queen's Own Highlander* is accelerating the 07.55 Kings Cross–Edinburgh away from its Newcastle stop.

On the delightful Northumberland coast at Scremerston, about 3 miles south of Berwick-upon-Tweed, and with Bamburgh Castle in the distance, on Tuesday 29 May 1979 a HST forming the 16.02 arrival at Berwick-upon-Tweed from Kings Cross is passing the site of Scremerston station, which closed in July 1951. In May 1979 northbound trains were terminating at Berwick-upon-Tweed following the collapse of Penmanshiel Tunnel in March 1979. Due to unstable ground the tunnel was unable to be reopened, necessitating a new alignment to be constructed. It did not open for about five months after the disaster, which killed two workmen.

The magnificent twenty-eight-arch Royal Border Bridge above the River Tweed on the approach to Berwick-upon-Tweed station. Deltic No. 55003 *Meld* is slowing for its stop heading the 15.00 Kings Cross–Edinburgh on Saturday 27 May 1978, about eleven years before this section of the East Coast Main Line was electrified. Berwick-upon-Tweed was the meeting place of the North Eastern Railway and the North British Railway, and at one time the River Tweed formed the border between England and Scotland. Now the border is at Marshall Meadows, almost 3 miles north of Berwick-upon-Tweed.

Meeting of English Electric power at Berwick-upon-Tweed on Sunday 28 May 1978. Deltic No. 55015 *Tulyar* is arriving for its stop with the 11.10 Edinburgh–Kings Cross as Class 40 No. 40147 eases out of the yard with a Down freight.